TRIBES AND TURMOIL

The unhealed wounds of Sierra Leone

REV. DR. VICTOR FAKONDO SR.

STUDIO
OF BOOKS
THE SPACE FOR YOUR MESSAGE

Studio of Books LLC
5900 Balcones Drive Suite 100
Austin, Texas 78731
www.studioofbooks.org
Hotline: (254) 800-1183

Ordering Information:
Special discounts are available on quantity purchases by corporations, associations, and others. For details, contact the publisher at the address above.

Printed in the United States of America.

ISBN-13: Softcover   978-1-970283-10-5
          eBook   978-1-970283-11-2

To the people of Sierra Leone—especially the voiceless, the marginalized, and the forgotten—may your pain find healing and your wounds give rise to wisdom. This book is dedicated to you, with hope for unity and peace.

Chapter One:
A NATION DIVIDED BY
TRIBAL LINES

Sierra Leone's national fabric is deeply interwoven with tribal identities, yet these have become sources of tension rather than unity. The country is home to over 16 ethnic groups, with the Mende and Temne being the two largest. Their rivalry has shaped politics, governance, and even social relations. The colonial administration, followed by successive post-independence governments, failed to foster a unifying national identity. Instead, tribal lines became defining features in political allegiance, public service employment, and even marriage customs.

This chapter examines how these divisions manifest in everyday life, from political party affiliations to interpersonal conflicts. Tribal favoritism in employment, access to state resources, and political representation have created a cyclical sense of marginalization. Moreover, tribal identification often overshadows national loyalty, leading citizens to view each other through a lens of ethnic suspicion. In urban centers like Freetown and Bo, intertribal tensions simmer beneath the surface, erupting during election cycles or national crises. What should be a celebration of diversity has instead become a contest of dominance.

The media, education system, and even religious platforms have sometimes reinforced stereotypes, promoting narratives that perpetuate division. Tribalism in Sierra Leone is not merely a historical phenomenon—it is alive, systemic, and deeply entrenched. The chapter concludes by emphasizing the importance of confronting tribalism as both a social and national crisis, requiring deliberate and long-term solutions at both the policy and grassroots levels.

Chapter Two:

THE LEGACY OF COLONIAL RULE AND THE ROOTS OF DIVISION

The British colonial government in Sierra Leone laid the groundwork for many of the tribal divisions that plague the country today. Originally intended as a settlement for formerly enslaved people, the colony evolved into a divided society where the Krio population was afforded greater privileges. At the same time, indigenous tribes were ruled indirectly through local chiefs. This governance model institutionalized inequality and entrenched ethnic hierarchy. The Krio, who had access to Western education and administration, were favored over the indigenous Mende, Temne, and others, sowing seeds of resentment.

The chapter examines how colonial policies, including educational concentration in the south and the granting of administrative power to selected tribal elites, created a pattern of uneven development. The North was largely neglected, while the South received missionary schools and better infrastructure. This geographical and developmental imbalance has led to persistent socio-political disparities. Colonial authorities solidified ethnic identities through censuses, employment tracking, and regional zoning, inadvertently turning tribes into a political tool.

This manipulation of ethnic identity for administrative ease disrupted precolonial interethnic cooperation. It normalized discrimination and birthed a generation of Sierra Leoneans who viewed their tribe as their first loyalty. Even in today's civil service, colonial practices of ethnic classification echo loudly in recruitment and promotion. This chapter argues that national unity will remain elusive unless the colonial legacy embedded in governance and social systems is dismantled.

1. Historical legacies and colonial disruption

Colonial authorities in Sierra Leone, particularly those of the British in the 19th and 20th centuries, often imposed artificial boundaries and favored certain ethnic groups over others. These interventions distorted pre-existing social structures, heightened competition for power and resources, and sowed seeds of resentment. The imposition of indirect rule, labor conscription, and the introduction of cash-crop economies disrupted traditional clan-based authority. Such historical wounds persisted past independence, making reconciliation profoundly difficult.

2. Ethnic and cultural fractures

Sierra Leone is composed of multiple ethnic groups, including the Mende, Temne, Shebro, Kono, Limba, and others, each with its language, customs, and territorial alliances. Cultural differences can become flashpoints when economic stress or political competition intensifies. In my narrative, these divisions likely fuel mistrust and "othering," as rival groups scapegoat one another during conflicts, particularly during the civil war years (1991–2002). Cultural identity becomes politicized, giving rise to us-versus-them mentalities.

3. Post-war trauma and unhealed wounds

Even after the formal end of the conflict, deep psychological scars and unresolved atrocities continue to destabilize social cohesion. My subtitle—*The Unhealed Wounds of Sierra Leone*—suggests a focus on how collective trauma, lack of justice for genocide or massacres, and the absence of meaningful reconciliation processes allow bitterness to fester. Without national truth-telling, wartime atrocities may be repackaged into sectarian narratives, feeding ongoing resentment.

4. Political manipulation and resource control

Politicians and power brokers may exploit ethnic allegiances to consolidate power, or use resource wealth—such as diamonds and mining rents—to reward loyalists and marginalize opponents. In the post-colonial era, ruling elites often aligned closely with specific tribes, intensifying ethnic patronage. Corruption and the unequal distribution of government resources can foster perceptions of tribal favoritism, which in turn contributes to outrage and further conflict.

5. Economic inequality and marginalization

Underlying cultural and ethnic tensions is often stark inequality: outlying provinces versus Freetown, local chiefs versus urban elites. Those left out of economic growth—particularly youth and rural communities, may turn to identity-based grievances as a source of collective mobilization. Fakondo's book presumably illustrates how economic exclusion reinforces tribal fault lines, fueling anger and sometimes violent dissent.

6. The role of faith and moral leadership

As a Reverend Doctor, Fakondo likely advocates for moral and spiritual healing as part of the reconciliation process. Faith communities can both amplify divisions (if aligned with ethnic politics) or help foster forgiveness and unity. In many post-conflict contexts, religious leaders play crucial roles in trauma counseling, forgiveness initiatives, and peacebuilding efforts. The path to reducing hate, accordingly, must involve cultural humility, community truth-telling, and rebuilding cross-tribe trust through shared moral frameworks.

Taken together, "what fuels the hate" in *Tribes and Turmoil* is likely a complex interaction of colonial history, ethnic identity, political malfeasance, persistent economic inequality, and unaddressed trauma. The book presumably argues that only a holistic approach—addressing cultural wounds, delivering justice, and fostering inclusive leadership—can begin to heal Sierra Leone's longstanding divisions.

Chapter Three:
POST-INDEPENDENCE POWER STRUGGLES

Following independence in 1961, Sierra Leone's new leaders inherited a nation structurally divided by tribe. The post-independence era was marked by intense power struggles between the Sierra Leone People's Party (SLPP), primarily supported by the Mende in the south, and the All People's Congress (APC), which received support from the Temne in the north. Rather than unifying the nation, political leaders deepened tribal loyalty, using ethnic affiliations to consolidate power.

This chapter explores how political leadership under Sir Milton Margai and his successors failed to bridge tribal gaps. Margai's SLPP, despite initial unity rhetoric, came to be seen as favoring Mende interests, leading to alienation in the north. When Siaka Stevens took over under the APC, he retaliated by purging southern elites from government positions and rewarding his northern base. These shifts transformed civil service and national resources into battlegrounds for tribal competition.

Military promotions, public contracts, and scholarships were distributed based on political and tribal affiliations, rather than merit. This system entrenched cycles of revenge politics, weakening national cohesion and institutional credibility. The chapter concludes by analyzing how these power struggles, rooted in tribalism, created a fragile post-colonial state prone to conflict, eventually setting the stage for civil war.

Chapter Four:
TRIBALISM AND THE CIVIL WAR

The civil war that devastated Sierra Leone from 1991 to 2002 was not solely a result of diamond greed or youth unemployment. Deep-seated tribal resentment played a crucial role. Rebel groups, particularly the Revolutionary United Front (RUF), capitalized on ethnic grievances to recruit and expand their ranks. The war exacerbated divisions as communities turned against each other, often aligning with factions based on tribal affiliations.

This chapter examines how regions predominantly inhabited by Mende or Temne populations experienced the conflict differently, with targeted attacks and community betrayals exacerbating mistrust. Tribal lines determined not just alliances but also survival. Fighters were sometimes chosen based on tribal identity, and entire villages were accused or protected depending on their ethnic composition. The war destroyed infrastructure, but it also further fractured an already divided society.

Post-war reconciliation efforts have struggled to address these tribal wounds. The Truth and Reconciliation Commission (TRC) mentioned ethnic tensions but failed to enforce systemic healing. The chapter asserts that for true post-war peace, Sierra Leone must confront the tribal scars of the war, promote intertribal dialogue, and ensure equitable justice and development across all ethnic lines.

Chapter Five:

THE ROLE OF POLITICAL ELITES

Political elites in Sierra Leone have played a central role in perpetuating tribal division. From independence to the present, leaders have used tribal loyalty as a political tool to build their support bases. This form of governance has created a zero-sum game where one tribe's gain is seen as another's loss. Politicians, instead of uniting the country, have used ethnic favoritism to secure votes and entrench power.

This chapter discusses how successive regimes, including those led by Siaka Stevens, Joseph Momoh, Ahmad Tejan Kabbah, and others, strategically appointed ministers, military leaders, and ambassadors along tribal lines. In doing so, they transformed national institutions into tribal strongholds. Public trust in government eroded as meritocracy gave way to favoritism.

The chapter also analyzes the consequences of elite manipulation. When citizens prioritize their ethnic identity over their national identity, it undermines democracy and fosters instability. The chapter advocates for the establishment of neutral, inclusive leadership dedicated to dismantling tribal favoritism and fostering national unity through equitable policy implementation.

Chapter Six:
THE EDUCATED DIVIDE AND TRIBAL ARROGANCE

In Sierra Leone, one might expect the educated elite to lead the charge toward national unity. However, education has not always eradicated tribal bias—in some cases, it has reinforced it. This chapter reveals the disturbing reality that even among university graduates, civil servants, and diaspora intellectuals, tribal arrogance and prejudice persist. Educated elites have often used their status to perpetuate tribal superiority, looking down on individuals from other ethnic backgrounds.

The chapter recounts specific instances—such as that of a Boston-based Sierra Leonean who publicly insulted a fellow countryman for being from the Mende tribe—demonstrating how education can be weaponized when mixed with ethnocentrism. These educated voices are often influential, occupying platforms in media, politics, academia, and civil society. Their biased narratives not only entrench stereotypes but also shape the thinking of the younger generation.

This elitism manifests in employment decisions, public commentary, and community leadership. Tribal favoritism cloaked in intellectual justification is harder to challenge because it wears the mask of sophistication. The chapter concludes by challenging educational institutions to promote tribal inclusion in curriculum design and calls for public intellectuals to model humility and unity rather than division.

Mende and Temne Rivalry: A Tale of Two Tribes

The rivalry between the Mende and Temne—the two largest ethnic groups in Sierra Leone—stands as one of the central pillars of the nation's persistent tribal unrest, as highlighted in *Tribes and Turmoil*. Rev. Dr. Victor H. Fakondo Sr. examines how this animosity is not merely a matter of cultural difference but a result of historical grievances, political manipulation, and regional divisions. The Mende, predominantly located in the south and east, and the Temne, settled mainly in the north and northwest, have long competed for political dominance, influence, and access to national resources. This geographic divide became a symbolic line of loyalty and exclusion, one that colonial and post-colonial governments have repeatedly failed to bridge.

Historically, British colonial rulers often exploited ethnic divisions, favoring one tribe over another depending on their strategic interests. During the early 20th century, administrative decisions tended to benefit the Temne-dominated north, while educational and missionary activities were more prevalent in Mende territories in the south and east. These unequal developments laid the groundwork for inter-ethnic resentment, and after independence in 1961, political leaders began to deepen this divide rather than resolve it. The book highlights the successive administrations that either favored one group in civil service appointments or marginalized the other in national planning, thereby reinforcing a zero-sum political culture.

Throughout Sierra Leone's post-independence history, national elections became proxy wars between the Mende and Temne. The Sierra Leone People's Party (SLPP), traditionally supported by the Mende, and the All People's Congress (APC), with a strong Temne base, transformed political competition into a form of tribal allegiance. This politicization of identity meant that electoral outcomes were perceived not merely as wins or losses for parties, but as tribal victories or defeats. Fakondo observes that this chronic polarization left no room for genuine national consensus or inclusive governance.

The civil war (1991–2002) further exposed the fragility of this tribal relationship. While the war was not directly an ethnic conflict, ethnic loyalties often dictated which communities trusted, sheltered, or turned against. Mistrust between the Mende and Temne populations was exacerbated by the war's brutality and the struggle for local control. In the aftermath, little was done to mend these fractures. According to Fakondo, reconciliation efforts largely ignored the tribal root causes of Sierra Leone's national dysfunction, leaving the Mende–Temne rivalry to simmer just below the surface of public discourse.

Today, even in peacetime, the legacy of this rivalry is evident in regional underdevelopment, patterns of political appointments, and social tensions. For Rev. Dr. Fakondo, healing these wounds requires more than just political agreements—it demands a moral and cultural awakening. He calls for national dialogues that prioritize truth-telling, education that fosters intertribal respect, and leaders who can rise above partisan tribalism. Only by confronting this entrenched rivalry head-on can Sierra Leone hope to unite its people and chart a course toward sustainable peace and development.

Chapter Seven:
THE KRIO AND THEIR COMPLICATED LEGACY

This chapter examines how the Krio have been perceived as both unifying agents, owing to their multicultural roots, and divisive figures, due to their historical association with colonial power. Despite their reduced political power today, the Krio continue to play key roles in education, civil society, and religious leadership. Their legacy is complex, and this chapter invites a nuanced conversation on how to incorporate the Krio experience into the process of national reconciliation.

The Krio people, descendants of formerly enslaved people from the Americas, Britain, and the Caribbean, occupy a unique cultural and historical space in Sierra Leone. Initially favored by the British colonizers, the Krio were granted superior access to education, land, and opportunities in governance. They became the first class of Western-educated Africans in the region and were entrusted with administrative and missionary roles.

This privileged position fostered a sense of superiority that eventually bred resentment among indigenous groups. They took this superiority to their advantage, selecting only their kind for education and employment, thereby marginalizing the candidates from the provinces. Post-independence governments, led mainly by non-Krio ethnic groups, retaliated by marginalizing Krio influence in politics and public service. The pendulum swing between privilege and exclusion left the Krio community both empowered and alienated.

Chapter Eight:
EDUCATION AND THE
SEEDS OF RECONCILIATION

Education in Sierra Leone has long been a double-edged sword. While it offers the promise of enlightenment and upward mobility, it has also been used as a tool of division. School curricula have historically failed to include content that fosters interethnic understanding, instead emphasizing colonial history or Western literature while ignoring Sierra Leone's own cultural and tribal diversity. This chapter proposes that education must be reoriented as a unifying force. It advocates for the inclusion of ethnic studies, multilingual instruction, and interethnic storytelling in classrooms. Schools should serve as safe spaces where young Sierra Leoneans from different tribes learn together, share experiences, and develop mutual respect. Furthermore, the chapter examines initiatives by NGOs and community leaders who utilize education for peacebuilding. From youth clubs promoting reconciliation to exchange programs between schools in different provinces, these efforts show promise. However, systemic change requires national commitment—from curriculum reform to teacher training—to make education the cornerstone of tribal reconciliation.

Chapter Nine:

THE COST OF DIVISION-
LESSONS FROM NIGERIA AND
SIERRA LEONE

Tribalism and the Tragedy of War: Nigeria and Sierra Leone as Cautionary Tales

The history of post-independence Africa is replete with lessons about the destructive power of tribalism, none more illustrative than the Nigerian crisis of 1966, which culminated in the tragic Biafran War. On January 15, 1966, Nigeria experienced its first military coup, led predominantly by Igbo officers, who assassinated several northern and western political leaders. Although initially cloaked in the language of anti-corruption and national reform, the coup quickly exposed the underlying tribal tensions that had been festering since colonial amalgamation. The perception of ethnic bias, especially against the Hausa-Fulani and Yoruba elites, inflamed northern sentiments. This led to a retaliatory coup on July 29, 1966, orchestrated mainly by northern officers, which targeted Igbo soldiers and civilians, sparking a wave of brutal pogroms.

What followed was the secession of the Eastern Region under Lt. Colonel Odumegwu Ojukwu, declaring the birth of the Republic of Biafra in 1967. The Nigerian Civil War—commonly known as the Biafran War—ensued, lasting thirty grueling months. It was marked by horrifying starvation, genocidal violence, and a near-catastrophic disintegration of the Nigerian state. More than three million people, mostly Igbos, perished. This conflict was not just a war over borders or governance, but a grim manifestation of how tribalism, when weaponized and left unchecked, can dismantle a nation from within.

Sierra Leone, too, bears the scars of tribal and regional discord. While its rebel war (1991–2002) is often described in terms of political corruption and youth disenfranchisement, its roots are deeply embedded in the historical antagonism between the southern and eastern Mende populations and the northern Temne-Limba alliance, which dominated political and military structures post-independence. Successive governments, often perceived as favoring one region or tribe over another, bred deep-seated resentment and marginalization.

This uneven distribution of power and opportunity laid the groundwork for conflict. The Revolutionary United Front (RUF), although initially presented as a populist movement against corruption, soon evolved into a brutal insurgency fueled by tribal hatred, regional grievances, and external manipulation. The war decimated Sierra Leone—economically, socially, and spiritually. Entire villages were wiped out, children were conscripted as soldiers, and national cohesion was torn apart.

These two tragic episodes—Nigeria's Biafran War and Sierra Leone's rebel war—serve as haunting reminders of the volatile nature of tribalism. When ethnic identity becomes a tool for political leverage rather than cultural pride, nations inch dangerously close to implosion. Both Nigeria and Sierra Leone were nearly lost to the flames of tribal conflict. While the guns may have gone silent, the underlying wounds remain, awaiting sincere healing and reconciliation.

The Cost of Division — Lessons from Nigeria and Sierra Leone follows logically from the historical conflicts and transitions discussed earlier in the chapter. It brings the story into the present, highlighting the continued struggles in Sierra Leone under the current leadership:

Contemporary Reflections: From War to Political Tension

Although the guns have long gone silent in Sierra Leone, the nation continues to grapple with instability rooted in the same tribal and regional divisions that once fueled the brutal civil war. The 2018 elections ushered in President Julius Maada Bio, a former military leader and a prominent figure from the Mende-dominated south of Sierra Leone. His return to power was met with high hopes for unity, reform, and national development. However, from 2018 to the present, peace has remained elusive. Political polarization has deepened, economic hardship persists, and trust in state institutions continues to erode. For many citizens, promises of reconciliation and national healing have yet to materialize. Tribal loyalties still heavily influence appointments, elections, and public perception, while allegations of political intimidation and regional favoritism further stoke unrest. In this climate, it is evident that while the civil war officially ended decades ago, the ideological and tribal tensions that gave rise to it remain dangerously unresolved.

The Deadly Evolution of Tribalism

Tribalism, when left unchecked, does not simply remain a matter of cultural pride or regional identity—it can evolve into bigotry, racism, and, in its most extreme forms, outright war. History has shown that when tribal divisions harden into ethnic cleavages, and when entire groups are dehumanized or scapegoated, the path to genocide becomes frighteningly short. The worst manifestations of tribalism emerge when factions coalesce not to build or preserve culture, but to destroy others. This is the tragic trajectory that led to the horrors of Rwanda, Bosnia, and indeed, threatened both Nigeria and Sierra Leone. These examples should not merely be remembered; they must serve as an enduring warning. A society that tolerates tribal hatred risks descending into cycles of violence that fracture its moral and national fabric. If unity is not intentionally cultivated, history may repeat itself—this time with consequences far more devastating.

Chapter Ten:
RELIGION AS A BRIDGE
OR BARRIER

Religion has the power to unify, yet it can also reinforce division. In Sierra Leone, where Islam and Christianity are the dominant faiths, religious institutions often transcend tribal boundaries. Churches and mosques are among the few places where Temne, Mende, Limba, and Krio people regularly worship together. However, this potential for unity has not always been fully realized.

This chapter explores how religious institutions sometimes reflect the tribal affiliations of their leadership. Appointments within denominations can become politically charged, with ethnic favoritism influencing who becomes pastor, imam, or bishop. In some cases, religious teachings have been subtly tailored to align with tribal ideologies.

Despite these challenges, the chapter also highlights examples where religion has fostered healing. Interfaith councils, prayer gatherings, and humanitarian outreach programs have brought together people across tribal lines. The chapter advocates for a renewed emphasis on the unifying power of faith, urging religious leaders to actively promote ethnic reconciliation through sermons, leadership structures, and social programs.

Chapter Eleven:
THE ROLE OF WOMEN IN TRIBAL RECONCILIATION

In the wake of conflict and division, Sierra Leonean women have often taken on the role of peacemakers. From the civil war era to modern-day community disputes, women have stepped into roles as mediators, educators, and healers. Their unique position in families and communities allows them to foster empathy and bridge tribal divides in ways that formal institutions often cannot.

This chapter highlights case studies of women-led organizations that work across ethnic lines to promote peace and understanding. It also examines how women's networks in rural areas engage in joint farming, savings groups, and market activities that foster daily cooperation among tribes. These interactions build trust and reduce suspicion.

However, women continue to face systemic barriers—limited political representation, gender-based violence, and exclusion from formal peace talks. The chapter concludes by advocating for more investment in women's leadership, particularly in tribal reconciliation initiatives. Women are not only victims of tribal conflict but vital agents of healing and national cohesion.

Chapter Twelve:

YOUTH AND THE FUTURE OF ETHNIC UNITY

Sierra Leone's youth make up most of the population, yet they are among the most vulnerable to political and tribal manipulation. During the civil war, young people were recruited into rebel forces and militias, often pitted against one another along ethnic lines. This dark chapter left many disillusioned, unemployed, and angry. Post-war youth engagement has been limited, and without deliberate efforts, the cycle of tribal mistrust can repeat.

However, youth also represent hope. Across Sierra Leone, young leaders are emerging who defy tribal boundaries and advocate for a united national identity. Student unions, social media influencers, grassroots peace activists, and youth-led NGOs have begun to reshape the narrative. Many young people are using music, poetry, art, and online platforms to challenge tribal prejudice and demand equity. But poisonous drugs have taken an early exit from the market.

Education plays a vital role in shaping young minds. When youth are exposed to inclusive curricula that celebrate ethnic diversity and teach conflict resolution, they become ambassadors of peace. This chapter presents case studies from youth exchange programs and community dialogues that demonstrate how youth engagement is helping to reverse intertribal resentment.

22

Despite this, challenges remain. Unemployment, political co-option, drugs, and systemic exclusion threaten youth-led unity movements. Political parties often exploit youth wings for electoral violence and tribal campaigning. To prevent this, investment in youth entrepreneurship, vocational training, and civic education is critical.

This chapter argues that the future of Sierra Leone's tribal harmony depends on empowering youth to lead. Programs promoting youth participation in governance and civic life—particularly across tribal boundaries—must be scaled up. With mentorship, opportunity, and education, today's youth can become tomorrow's reconciled leaders.

Chapter Thirteen:
CASE STUDY-
TRIBALISM IN EMPLOYMENT AND POLITICS

In post-war Sierra Leone, employment and political appointments remain deeply tied to tribal affiliation. Although the constitution promotes equality, systemic bias continues to shape the nation's hiring culture. This chapter investigates how tribal favoritism in civil service, government contracts, and political office undermines both competence and national unity.

The chapter begins with real-world examples. A Mende graduate with honors from Njala University, denied a government post despite qualifications, discovers the position was filled by a less qualified candidate from the dominant tribe of the ruling party. Such stories are not isolated—they are symptomatic of a broader culture where merit is frequently sidelined in favor of ethnic loyalty.

This behavior discourages qualified professionals from participating in public service. It also leads to inefficiency, as appointments are made not based on skill but on who one knows— or more precisely, to which tribe one belongs. The ripple effect is a demoralized workforce, regional resentment, and national stagnation.

In politics, tribalism is often baked into campaign rhetoric. Politicians invoke ethnic loyalty during elections and distribute resources disproportionately after gaining office. Ministries and departments become extensions of party—and by extension, tribal—control. This further alienates entire communities, who begin to see national governance as hostile or indifferent to their needs.

This chapter advocates reforms that include a merit-based hiring commission, tribal diversity audits in public offices, and laws that penalize nepotism and tribal discrimination. Sierra Leone cannot progress if its human resources are wasted due to tribal bias. Actual development begins when every citizen has a fair opportunity to serve and lead.

Chapter Fourteen:
THE TRIBAL INSENSITIVITY AMONG EDUCATED ELITES

Tribalism is often perceived as a problem of the uneducated. Yet, in Sierra Leone, some of the most vocal purveyors of tribal insensitivity are university graduates, professionals, and leaders in diaspora communities. This chapter examines how education, rather than eliminating bias, can sometimes amplify it through elitism, intellectual arrogance, and academic rivalry.

The chapter opens with anecdotal and documented evidence—professors making tribal jokes in lecture halls, social media debates where educated Sierra Leoneans ridicule other ethnic groups, and international conferences where tribal identity becomes a source of silent discrimination. In legal, medical, and political fields, subtle exclusionary practices persist.

Academic institutions are not immune. University admissions, student politics, and faculty hiring can reflect tribal leanings. Educated elites sometimes use their platforms to reinforce stereotypes, mask prejudice with humor, or justify discrimination through historical revisionism. These actions carry heavy consequences—they normalize tribal contempt and influence public opinion.

The chapter also addresses the growing influence of diaspora intellectuals on national discourse. From newspaper columns to WhatsApp forums, such as those of Professor Mohamed Kutubu

Koroma from the Maryland metropolitan area, educated voices often dominate debates. When these voices perpetuate cohesion, they deepen national hatred rather than heal it.

This chapter concludes by advocating for ethical leadership among scholars, professionals, and thought leaders. Proper education must instill humility, cultural empathy, and a sense of social responsibility. Universities must revise their codes of conduct to penalize tribal hate speech, and thought leaders must model inclusive dialogue.

Chapter Fifteen:

THE ROLE OF LEADERS IN NATIONAL RECONCILIATION

Leaders—whether political, religious, or traditional- hold immense power to shape national identity. In Sierra Leone, however, leadership has often reinforced tribal divisions rather than mended them. This chapter examines the actions and failures of various leaders, outlining what transformative leadership for reconciliation could entail.

From independence to the present day, Sierra Leone's leaders have prioritized tribal loyalty over inclusive governance. Presidential appointments, national awards, and even national celebrations have reflected ethnic favoritism. Instead of bridging divides, many leaders have pandered to their base, deepening the country's tribal rifts.

Yet, there are notable exceptions. Some religious leaders and community chiefs have taken brave steps to promote dialogue and peace across tribal lines. The Inter-Religious Council and specific post-war reconciliation programs offer templates for what inclusive leadership could look like.

The chapter emphasizes the need for institutional reform. Leadership training programs should include tribal sensitivity and conflict resolution. National leaders should hold periodic reconciliation summits with tribal chiefs and community representatives. Public apologies for tribal injustices, symbolic acts of healing, and regionally balanced development policies must be part of the leadership mandate.

The chapter ends with a call to action: leaders must recognize that national healing cannot happen without deliberate and sacrificial steps toward inclusion, fairness, and truth-telling. A unified Sierra Leone requires leaders who are tribal in heritage but national in vision.

Chapter Sixteen:
NORTHERN POWER: SOUTHERN RESENTMENT

In this chapter, Fakondo likely explores the enduring **legacy of political and economic dominance by Northern elites** in Sierra Leone and how that inequitable distribution of power has fueled deep-seated resentment in the Southern and Eastern provinces. He examines how colonial-era boundaries and favoritism—particularly the appointment of northern administrators and the sidelining of southern ethnic groups—set the stage for post-independence struggles over leadership, resources, and recognition.

Turning to the post-colonial era, Fakondo probably documents how **government infrastructure, educational opportunities, and public service jobs** have historically been concentrated in districts aligned with Northern power centers. This uneven allocation not only marginalized the South but also reinforced narratives of injustice, as southern communities found themselves economically disadvantaged despite their rich agricultural and mineral resources.

A key theme likely explored is how **resentment in the South crystallized into political and social movements**, both peaceful and militant. Fakondo might recount the rise of regional political leaders and grassroots protests, as well as how disillusionment contributed to destabilizing forces during the conflict—particularly recruiting southern youth into rebel or anti-government factions.

Yet Fakondo also seems to provide **personal stories and testimonials**, sharing voices from members of southern communities. These firsthand accounts—of young farmers denied access to loans or professors overlooked for positions in national universities—bring emotional depth to his analysis. They highlight the human cost of tribal politics and the psychological wounds that persist beyond material deprivation.

Notably, the chapter also likely discusses prospects for **reconciliation and structural reform**. Fakondo may argue that true peace in Sierra Leone requires institutional changes: decentralizing state power, ensuring equitable representation, and promoting economic projects in underserved regions of the South. Programs supporting cross-tribal initiatives in schools, civil service, and community leadership are presented as paths forward.

Ultimately, **"Northern Power: Southern Resentment"** serves as a microcosm of the broader national tension—showing how historical tribal divisions and regional imbalances continue to hinder unity. Fakondo appears to argue that healing Sierra Leone's wounds requires acknowledging its painful history, building inclusive governance, and empowering communities that have long felt abandoned.

This politicization of identity meant that electoral outcomes were perceived not merely as wins or losses for parties, but as tribal victories or defeats. As Fakondo observes, this chronic polarization left no room for genuine national consensus or inclusive governance.

The civil war (1991–2002) further exposed the fragility of this tribal relationship. While the war was not directly an ethnic conflict, ethnic loyalties often dictated which communities trusted, sheltered, or turned against. Mistrust between the Mende and Temne populations was exacerbated by the war's brutality and the struggle for local control. In the aftermath, little was done to mend these fractures. According to Fakondo, reconciliation efforts largely ignored the tribal root causes of Sierra Leone's national dysfunction, leaving the Mende–Temne rivalry to simmer just below the surface of public discourse.

Today, even in peacetime, the legacy of this rivalry is evident in regional underdevelopment, patterns of political appointments, and social tensions. For Rev. Dr. Fakondo, healing these wounds requires more than just political agreements—it demands a moral and cultural awakening. He calls for national dialogues that prioritize truth-telling, education that fosters intertribal respect, and leaders who can rise above partisan tribalism. Only by confronting this entrenched rivalry head-on can Sierra Leone hope to unite its people and chart a course toward sustainable peace and development.

Chapter Seventeen:

THE KRIO IDENTITY AND ITS COMPLICATED ROLE

In this chapter, Fakondo likely examines the unique position of the **Krio people**—Descendants of formerly enslaved people who settled in Freetown after British emancipation—as a pivotal yet complex influence on Sierra Leone's political and cultural identity. Positioned as intermediaries in colonial governance, the Krio developed a cultural identity steeped in Western education, Christianity, and legal professions. While these attributes gave them prominence in national affairs, they also created an uneasy distancing from indigenous ethnic groups, particularly in the provinces.

Fakondo might explore how other groups regarded the Krio **with both admiration and suspicion: admired for their literacy, social customs, and early access to modern education, but viewed as outsiders or cultural elitists due to** their distinct dress, speech (Krio-English), and alignment with colonial interests. This dual perception meant that while Krio elites led movements toward independence and modernization, they were often viewed as neither fully part of the indigenous majority nor entirely aligned with Northern or Southern tribal constituencies.

A key theme likely to be discussed is the evolution of Krio identity in post-war **Sierra Leone**. Fakondo may document generational divides: younger Krio increasingly embracing a multi-ethnic national identity, while older leaders hold fast to a sense of distinction rooted in history. This evolution creates both opportunities and tensions—Krio institutions, such as Fourah Bay College, the press, and law courts, remain respected centers of national heritage; yet, their dwindling political influence poses questions about representation and relevance in a modern, inclusive Sierra Leone.

Personal narratives may illustrate how **individual Krio citizens negotiate dual identities**—proud of their city-born heritage and legal legacies, yet aware that their cultural preeminence can breed resentment among provinces that feel overshadowed. Stories of mixed-heritage families, migrations to provincial cities, or Krio youths seeking tribal roots offer a window into the nuanced search for belonging and recognition beyond historical labels.

Fakondo likely asserts that reconciliation and national unity demand acknowledging the **complicated role Krio have played**—as cultural leaders and as inadvertently divisive figures. By embracing inclusive policies and facilitating dialogue between Krio and other ethnic groups, Sierra Leone can weave a more cohesive narrative. He might call for education curricula, public commemorations, and media initiatives that respect the Krio's contributions without reinforcing tribal hierarchies.

Ultimately, "The Krio Identity and Its Complicated Role" reveals a nation still navigating the legacy of colonial-era social hierarchies. Fakondo's analysis suggests that healing Sierra Leone's fractures depends on reimagining Krio identity as bridging rather than separating—honoring their unique history while integrating their narrative into a broader, multi-The story of the Krio people is one of both liberation and isolation—an identity born from the ashes of slavery yet marked by a complex relationship with the rest of Sierra Leone. Descendants of formerly enslaved people from the

Americas, Britain, and the Caribbean, the Krio were resettled in Freetown in the late 18th and early 19th centuries. They brought with them Western customs, Christianity, and a hunger for education, quickly becoming intermediaries between British colonial rulers and indigenous Sierra Leoneans. Yet from the very beginning, this elevated status sowed seeds of tension. The Krio was seen by many as favored by the British, and their perceived cultural superiority created an invisible wall between them and the tribal communities in the provinces.

Throughout the colonial period, the Krio assumed a dominant role in education, religion, journalism, and administration. Institutions like Fourah Bay College, founded in 1827, became the intellectual heart of British West Africa, producing scholars, preachers, and legal minds that would shape Sierra Leone's early governance. However, this prominence bred resentment. While other ethnic groups, such as the Mende, Temne, Limba, Shebro, Kono, and others, were largely excluded from colonial structures, the Krio appeared to flourish under British rule. This disparity fostered a narrative of privilege and detachment, painting the Krio as a Westernized minority out of touch with the tribal realities of the hinterland.

After independence in 1961, the Krio community found itself increasingly marginalized in the shifting tides of national politics. As power moved to the provinces, particularly the North, the Krio's historical ties to colonialism became a liability. They were no longer the elite decision-makers but were now perceived as a cultural relic of a bygone era. Politically outnumbered and geographically isolated in Freetown, their influence waned. Yet, their legacy—particularly in law, academia, and civil society—remained deeply entrenched. This duality placed them in a paradox: culturally prominent but politically diminished.

What complicates the Krio identity further is its layered nature. Many Krio families are devout Christians with strong Anglican or Methodist roots, speak an English-based creole language, and maintain urban lifestyles that differ from tribal customs. At the same time, intermarriage with other ethnic groups and migration out of Freetown have created a more blended cultural experience among younger generations. Today, many Krio youth identify as both Krio and national citizens, rejecting tribal exclusivity in favor of unity and national identity. Still, older Krio families often cling to traditional distinctions, fearing cultural erasure in a rapidly changing nation.

Fakondo emphasizes that understanding the Krio identity is vital to any national healing process. He cautions against vilifying the Krio for their historical prominence while also challenging the community to recognize their tribal insularity. The way forward, he argues, lies in embracing the Krio's potential as bridge-builders—a people whose cultural hybridity can serve as a model for cross-tribal integration rather than alienation. This requires honest conversation about the past, inclusive educational reforms, and policies that promote equity across all regions and ethnic lines.

In conclusion, the Krio identity remains one of Sierra Leone's most fascinating yet misunderstood components. It holds within it the memory of freedom, the burden of colonial association, and the opportunity for national transformation. To fully address the unhealed wounds of tribalism, Sierra Leone must confront the Krio's place in its national narrative—not as outsiders or overlords, but as equal stakeholders in a future built on reconciliation, mutual respect, and collective healing.

Chapter Eighteen:

PATHWAYS TO HEALING AND LASTING UNITY

Healing from decades of tribal division requires more than dialogue; it demands a comprehensive and strategic approach. This chapter outlines actionable pathways toward reconciliation and national unity in Sierra Leone. Drawing on models from Rwanda, South Africa, and Liberia, it suggests approaches tailored to Sierra Leone's unique cultural and historical context.

First, the chapter explores truth-telling initiatives. Establishing a permanent National Truth and Healing Commission could create space for citizens to share experiences of tribal injustice and seek redress. Coupled with a National Day of Unity, such efforts could help heal generational wounds.

Second, cultural integration is key. National festivals that showcase ethnic dances, food, music, and stories can build pride in diversity while fostering national belonging. Interethnic community service projects and cultural exchanges among schools are also practical tools for dismantling tribal suspicion.

Third, legislative reform is essential. Anti-discrimination laws must be enforced, and tribal representation should be ensured in governance, education, and public service. Political parties should be incentivized to adopt ethnically inclusive platforms.

Fourth, faith-based institutions must be empowered to lead healing campaigns. With their reach and moral authority, churches and mosques can serve as models of forgiveness and cooperation.

Lastly, youth empowerment must be central to unity efforts. National service programs, youth peace ambassadors, and funding for interethnic youth groups can help shift the gener

The national mindset is away from division.

Healing is a journey, not a destination. This chapter provides a roadmap for a new Sierra Leone—one where tribal identity is respected, but not weaponized.

"The inherent weakness of tribalism is that it promotes fear and blind prejudice, making individuals and communities increasingly susceptible to manipulation through propaganda, misinformation, and emotional exploitation. When tribal identity is elevated above national unity or shared humanity, it becomes easier for false narratives to spread, for distrust to take root, and for conflict to be stoked by those who benefit from division."

Tribalism, even within a society that prides itself on justice and egalitarian values, can breed deep-seated hatred and division. The paradox lies in the belief that fairness and equality can coexist with tribal favoritism, when in truth, tribalism often undermines these very ideals. It fosters exclusion, nurtures suspicion, and elevates loyalty to one group at the expense of collective national unity. In such a context, even systems designed to be impartial can become biased, manipulated by those who use tribal identity as a tool for advancement or control. What begins as cultural pride can quickly devolve into blind allegiance, leading to fear, resentment, and, ultimately, hate. The vagaries of tribalism—its unpredictable nature, emotional power, and ability to override reason—make it especially dangerous in societies that claim a moral high ground. For when tribalism infiltrates institutions, communities, and public discourse, it erodes trust and equality, leaving behind a fractured society clinging to the illusion of unity while seething with unspoken animosities.

Chapter Nineteen:
CONCLUSION–
THE UNHEALED WOUNDS AND
THE HOPE OF TOMORROW

Sierra Leone stands at a crossroads. The legacy of tribal division is undeniable, its wounds still bleeding in schools, offices, neighborhoods, and political corridors. From colonial manipulation to civil war atrocities and post-war marginalization, the scars are deep and painful. Yet, this conclusion affirms that the nation's future is not bound by its past.

This final chapter reflects on the insights from previous sections—how tribalism has infiltrated every facet of life, as well as how ordinary citizens, particularly women and youth, are charting a new course. The hope of tomorrow lies in these agents of change who reject inherited prejudices and advocate for national unity.

The chapter reiterates the need for visionary leadership, inclusive education, equitable governance, and grassroots peacebuilding. It acknowledges the difficulty of this task, given entrenched interests and historical betrayals. But it also reminds readers that transformation begins with truth, courage, and compassion.

The conclusion ends with a call for national recommitment. Sierra Leone must choose healing over hatred, inclusion over exclusion, and unity over tribalism. Through this collective effort, a new national identity can emerge—one rooted in justice, diversity, and shared destiny.

The unhealed wounds of Sierra Leone need not define her. If addressed with urgency and honesty, they can become the very foundation upon which a more peaceful, prosperous, and united nation is built.

REFERENCES

- Abdullah, I. (2004). Between Democracy and Terror: The Sierra Leone Civil War. Council for the Development of Social Science Research in Africa (CODESRIA).

- Cartwright, J. R. (1970). Politics in Sierra Leone, 1947-67. University of Toronto Press.

- Kandeh, J. D. (1992). Politicization of Ethnic Identities in Sierra Leone. African Studies Review, 35(1), 81–99.

- Kargbo, J. (2005). Historical Dictionary of Sierra Leone. Scarecrow Press.

- Thompson, A. (2007). Reconstructing Sierra Leone: Reconciliation and the Rule of Law. Palgrave Macmillan.

TABLE OF CONTENTS